# The MAILBOX

The Education Center

# Math ENVELOPE Centers

MW00450813

**15 READY-TO-USE CENTERS**

- **Addition and Subtraction Facts**

- **Two- and Three-Digit Addition**

- **Two- and Three-Digit Subtraction**

- **Multiplication Facts**

- **Two-Digit by One-Digit Multiplication**

- **Multiplication and Division Fact Families**

- **Comparing Numbers to 1,000**

- **Place Value**

- **Equivalent Fractions**

- **Coin Combinations to $1.00**

- **Time to the Half Hour and Quarter Hour**

- **Linear Measurement**

Build Basic Math Skills!

**Managing Editor:** Hope Taylor Spencer

**Editorial Team:** Becky S. Andrews, Kimberley Bruck, Karen P. Shelton, Diane Badden, Thad H. McLaurin, Debra Liverman, Jennifer Bragg, Karen A. Brudnak, Hope Rodgers, Dorothy C. McKinney

**Production Team:** Lisa K. Pitts, Pam Crane, Rebecca Saunders, Jennifer Tipton Cappoen, Chris Curry, Sarah Foreman, Theresa Lewis Goode, Clint Moore, Greg D. Rieves, Barry Slate, Donna K. Teal, Zane Williard, Tazmen Carlisle, Marsha Heim, Lynette Dickerson, Mark Rainey

www.themailbox.com

## Another Fine Product From the Learning Centers Club®

# Table of Contents

# 15 Envelope Centers

## Skills

Manufactured in China
10 9 8 7 6 5 4 3 2 1

# How to Use

1. Read the teacher page for each envelope center and prepare the center as directed.

2. Use the activity as independent practice at a math center or have the student complete the activity at her seat. These centers are the perfect solution for early finishers. If desired, send a center home with a student for additional practice.

3. Use the checklist on page 4 to help keep track of each student's progress.

**Envelope Center**

# Envelope Center Checklist

| Student | Pajama Party: Addition and subtraction facts to 18 | Pampered Pups: Adding two-digit numbers without regrouping | "Ssssend" Me a Letter! Adding three-digit numbers with one regrouping | Sunny-Day Fun: Subtracting two-digit numbers without regrouping | Cleanup Crew: Subtracting three-digit numbers with one regrouping | Cricket's Cupcakes: Multiplication facts 0–5 | Team Photo: Multiplication facts 6–10 | Stocking Up: Multiplying two-digit numbers by one-digit numbers | What a Ride! Relating multiplication and division | What's for Lunch? Comparing numbers to 1,000 | Surf's Up! Identifying place value | Dinner for Two: Equivalent fractions | Money Tree: Coin combinations to $1.00 | Tee Time: Telling time to the half hour and quarter hour | Camp Big Bear: Measuring to the nearest centimeter |
|---|---|---|---|---|---|---|---|---|---|---|---|---|---|---|---|
| | | | | | | | | | | | | | | | |
| | | | | | | | | | | | | | | | |
| | | | | | | | | | | | | | | | |
| | | | | | | | | | | | | | | | |
| | | | | | | | | | | | | | | | |
| | | | | | | | | | | | | | | | |
| | | | | | | | | | | | | | | | |
| | | | | | | | | | | | | | | | |
| | | | | | | | | | | | | | | | |
| | | | | | | | | | | | | | | | |
| | | | | | | | | | | | | | | | |
| | | | | | | | | | | | | | | | |
| | | | | | | | | | | | | | | | |
| | | | | | | | | | | | | | | | |
| | | | | | | | | | | | | | | | |
| | | | | | | | | | | | | | | | |
| | | | | | | | | | | | | | | | |
| | | | | | | | | | | | | | | | |
| | | | | | | | | | | | | | | | |
| | | | | | | | | | | | | | | | |
| | | | | | | | | | | | | | | | |
| | | | | | | | | | | | | | | | |
| | | | | | | | | | | | | | | | |
| | | | | | | | | | | | | | | | |
| | | | | | | | | | | | | | | | |
| | | | | | | | | | | | | | | | |

# Pajama Party

### Pages 5–12

## Materials:

scissors
glue
10" x 13" envelope

## Preparing the center:

1. Tear out the student directions, center mat, and center strips on pages 7–12.
2. Glue the student directions (page 7) on the envelope. If desired, laminate the center mat and strips on pages 9–12.
3. Cut out the strips. Cut the slits on the mat. Thread one strip through the mat.
4. Make copies of the recording sheet on page 6.
5. Store the center mat, extra strip, and copies of the recording sheet inside the envelope. If desired, also include a copy of the answer key card on page 125 for self-checking.

Addition and subtraction facts to 18

**Pajama Party**

Here's what you do:
1. Slide the strip to A.
2. Copy the problem onto the recording sheet.
3. Solve.
4. Slide the strip and repeat.

| Strip 2 |
| --- |
| A. 7 + 9 = |
| B. 14 – 7 = |
| C. 11 – 7 = |
| D. 8 + 7 = |
| E. 18 – 9 = |
| F. 5 + 6 = |
| G. 16 – 8 = |
| H. 9 + 5 = |
| I. 13 – 7 = |
| J. 6 + 6 = |
| K. 8 + 9 = |
| L. 15 – 6 = |

A. 9 + 8 =

| |
| --- |
| F. 9 + 7 = |
| G. 15 – 8 = |
| H. 10 – 7 = |
| I. 6 + 9 = |
| J. 9 + 9 = |
| K. 14 – 8 = |
| L. 7 + 5 = |

Name **Sara**

**Pajama Party**

Addition and subtraction facts to 18

A. 9 + 8 = 17
B.
C.
D.
E.
F.
G.
H.
I.
J.
K.
L.

**6** Name _____

# Pajama Party

SQUIRREL POOL

A. ___ ___ = ___
B. ___ ___ = ___
C. ___ ___ = ___
D. ___ ___ = ___
E. ___ ___ = ___
F. ___ ___ = ___
G. ___ ___ = ___
H. ___ ___ = ___
I. ___ ___ = ___
J. ___ ___ = ___
K. ___ ___ = ___
L. ___ ___ = ___

**Note to the teacher:** Use with the directions on page 5.

# Pajama Party

**Here's what you do:**

1. Slide the strip to A.

2. Copy the problem onto the recording sheet.

3. Solve.

4. Slide the strip and repeat.

# Pajama Party

## Strip 1

A. $9 + 8 =$

B. $12 - 8 =$

C. $7 + 7 =$

D. $11 - 6 =$

E. $17 - 9 =$

F. $9 + 7 =$

G. $15 - 8 =$

H. $10 - 7 =$

I. $6 + 9 =$

J. $9 + 9 =$

K. $14 - 8 =$

L. $7 + 5 =$

## Strip 2

A. $7 + 9 =$

B. $14 - 7 =$

C. $11 - 7 =$

D. $8 + 7 =$

E. $18 - 9 =$

F. $5 + 6 =$

G. $16 - 8 =$

H. $9 + 5 =$

I. $13 - 7 =$

J. $6 + 6 =$

K. $8 + 9 =$

L. $15 - 6 =$

Pajama Party
TEC61032

Pajama Party
TEC61032

# Pampered Pups

## Pages 13–20

### Materials:

scissors
glue
10" x 13" envelope
resealable plastic bag

### Preparing the center:

1. Tear out the student directions, center mat, and center cards on pages 15–20.
2. Glue the student directions (page 15) on the envelope. If desired, laminate the center mat and cards on pages 17–20.
3. Cut out the cards and place them in the bag.
4. Make copies of the reproducible recording sheet on page 14.
5. Store the center mat, bag, and copies of the recording sheeet inside the envelope. If desired, also include a copy of the answer key card on page 125 for self-checking.

# Pampered Pups

Write and solve each problem on the cards in its matching box.

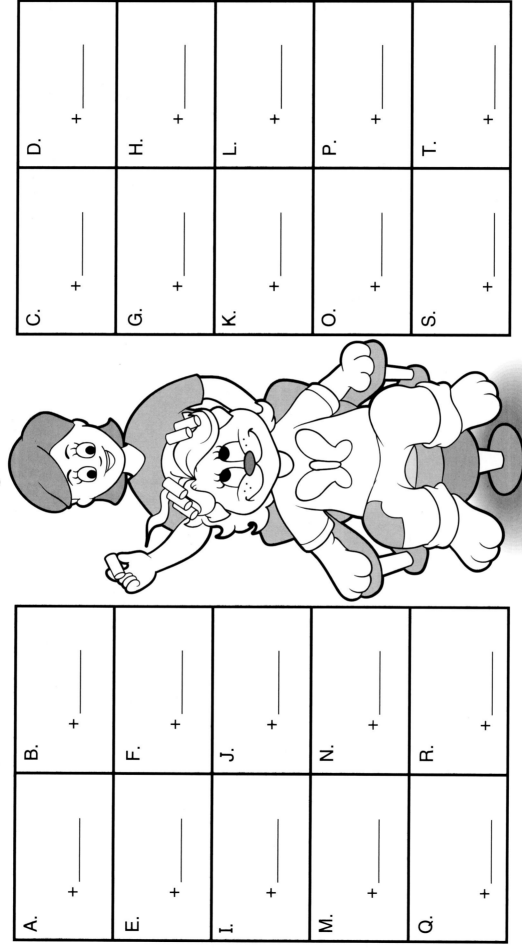

| | |
|---|---|
| A. ___ + ___ ——— | B. ___ + ___ ——— |
| E. ___ + ___ ——— | F. ___ + ___ ——— |
| I. ___ + ___ ——— | J. ___ + ___ ——— |
| M. ___ + ___ ——— | N. ___ + ___ ——— |
| Q. ___ + ___ ——— | R. ___ + ___ ——— |

| | |
|---|---|
| C. ___ + ___ ——— | D. ___ + ___ ——— |
| G. ___ + ___ ——— | H. ___ + ___ ——— |
| K. ___ + ___ ——— | L. ___ + ___ ——— |
| O. ___ + ___ ——— | P. ___ + ___ ——— |
| S. ___ + ___ ——— | T. ___ + ___ ——— |

**Note to the teacher:** Use with the directions on page 13.

# Pampered Pups

## Here's what you do:

1. Take a card.

2. Solve the problem on your recording sheet.

3. Decide whether the card is correct.

4. Put it on the matching tub.

5. Repeat.

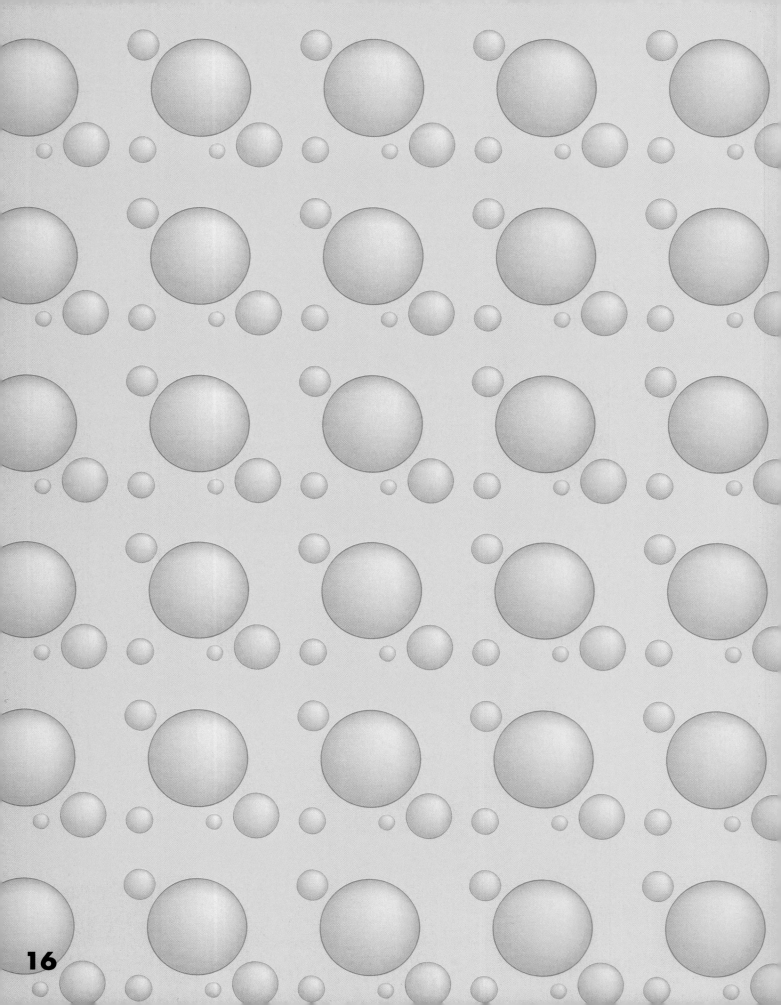

pampered pups

Incorrect

Correct

# Pampered Pups

| | | | |
|---|---|---|---|
| **A.** $\begin{array}{r} 25 \\ + 43 \\ \hline 68 \end{array}$ | **B.** $\begin{array}{r} 37 \\ + 61 \\ \hline 98 \end{array}$ | **C.** $\begin{array}{r} 30 \\ + 40 \\ \hline 70 \end{array}$ | **D.** $\begin{array}{r} 84 \\ + 14 \\ \hline 88 \end{array}$ |
| **E.** $\begin{array}{r} 31 \\ + 56 \\ \hline 87 \end{array}$ | **F.** $\begin{array}{r} 25 \\ + 20 \\ \hline 55 \end{array}$ | **G.** $\begin{array}{r} 23 \\ + 71 \\ \hline 94 \end{array}$ | **H.** $\begin{array}{r} 41 \\ + 52 \\ \hline 83 \end{array}$ |
| **I.** $\begin{array}{r} 60 \\ + 15 \\ \hline 75 \end{array}$ | **J.** $\begin{array}{r} 21 \\ + 31 \\ \hline 52 \end{array}$ | **K.** $\begin{array}{r} 34 \\ + 20 \\ \hline 64 \end{array}$ | **L.** $\begin{array}{r} 54 \\ + 11 \\ \hline 65 \end{array}$ |
| **M.** $\begin{array}{r} 63 \\ + 33 \\ \hline 96 \end{array}$ | **N.** $\begin{array}{r} 21 \\ + 58 \\ \hline 77 \end{array}$ | **O.** $\begin{array}{r} 10 \\ + 40 \\ \hline 50 \end{array}$ | **P.** $\begin{array}{r} 46 \\ + 22 \\ \hline 67 \end{array}$ |
| **Q.** $\begin{array}{r} 12 \\ + 36 \\ \hline 48 \end{array}$ | **R.** $\begin{array}{r} 21 \\ + 15 \\ \hline 36 \end{array}$ | **S.** $\begin{array}{r} 50 \\ + 43 \\ \hline 83 \end{array}$ | **T.** $\begin{array}{r} 75 \\ + 23 \\ \hline 98 \end{array}$ |

| Pampered Pups<br>TEC61032 | Pampered Pups<br>TEC61032 | Pampered Pups<br>TEC61032 | Pampered Pups<br>TEC61032 |
|---|---|---|---|
| Pampered Pups<br>TEC61032 | Pampered Pups<br>TEC61032 | Pampered Pups<br>TEC61032 | Pampered Pups<br>TEC61032 |
| Pampered Pups<br>TEC61032 | Pampered Pups<br>TEC61032 | Pampered Pups<br>TEC61032 | Pampered Pups<br>TEC61032 |
| Pampered Pups<br>TEC61032 | Pampered Pups<br>TEC61032 | Pampered Pups<br>TEC61032 | Pampered Pups<br>TEC61032 |
| Pampered Pups<br>TEC61032 | Pampered Pups<br>TEC61032 | Pampered Pups<br>TEC61032 | Pampered Pups<br>TEC61032 |

# "Ssssend" Me a Letter!

### Pages 21–28

## Materials:

scissors
glue
10" x 13" envelope
resealable plastic bag

## Preparing the center:

1. Tear out the student directions, center mat, and center cards on pages 23–28.
2. Glue the student directions (page 23) on the envelope. If desired, laminate the center mat and cards on pages 25–28.
3. Cut apart the cards and place them in the bag.
4. Make copies of the reproducible recording sheet on page 22.
5. Store the center mat, bag, and copies of the recording sheet inside the envelope. If desired, include a copy of the answer key card on page 125 for self-checking.

Name _____

# "Ssssend" Me a Letter!

| | | | |
|---|---|---|---|
| A.<br><br>  + _____ | B.<br><br>  + _____ | C.<br><br>  + _____ | D.<br><br>  + _____ |
| E.<br><br>  + _____ | F.<br><br>  + _____ | G.<br><br>  + _____ | H.<br><br>  + _____ |
| I.<br><br>  + _____ | J.<br><br>  + _____ | K.<br><br>  + _____ | L.<br><br>  + _____ |
| M.<br><br>  + _____ | N.<br><br>  + _____ | O.<br><br>  + _____ | P.<br><br>  + _____ |
| Q.<br><br>  + _____ | R.<br><br>  + _____ | | |
| S.<br><br>  + _____ | T.<br><br>  + _____ | | |

**Note to the teacher:** Use with the directions on page 21.

# "Ssssend" Me a Letter!

## Here's what you do:

1. Take a letter card.

2. Solve the problem on the recording sheet.

3. Put the letter card on the matching box.

4. Repeat.

"Sssssend" Me a Letter!

| 795 ⊙ | 869 ⊙ | 309 ⊙ | 808 ⊙ | 783 ⊙ |
| 963 ⊙ | 947 ⊙ | 872 ⊙ | 601 ⊙ | 976 ⊙ |
| 519 ⊙ | 928 ⊙ | 515 ⊙ | 647 ⊙ | 916 ⊙ |
| 049 ⊙ | 716 ⊙ | 994 ⊙ | 483 ⊙ | 819 ⊙ |

# "Ssssend" Me a Letter

Center Cards
Use with the directions on page 21.

| | | | | |
|---|---|---|---|---|
| **A.** 260 + 341 | **B.** 648 + 147 | **C.** 223 + 596 | **D.** 567 + 361 | **E.** 438 + 525 |
| **F.** 304 + 479 | **G.** 175 + 472 | **H.** 638 + 356 | **I.** 391 + 478 | **J.** 435 + 205 |
| **K.** 528 + 419 | **L.** 244 + 271 | **M.** 412 + 396 | **N.** 281 + 435 | **O.** 637 + 235 |
| **P.** 122 + 187 | **Q.** 319 + 164 | **R.** 158 + 361 | **S.** 758 + 218 | **T.** 176 + 740 |

**27**

**"Ssssend" Me a Letter!**
TEC61032

**"Ssssend" Me a Letter!**
TEC61032

**"Ssssend" Me a Letter!**
TEC61032

**"Ssssend" Me a Letter!**
TEC61032

**"Ssssend" Me a Letter!**
TEC61032

**"Ssssend" Me a Letter!**
TEC61032

**"Ssssend" Me a Letter!**
TEC61032

**"Ssssend" Me a Letter!**
TEC61032

**"Ssssend" Me a Letter!**
TEC61032

**"Ssssend" Me a Letter!**
TEC61032

**"Ssssend" Me a Letter!**
TEC61032

**"Ssssend" Me a Letter!**
TEC61032

**"Ssssend" Me a Letter!**
TEC61032

**"Ssssend" Me a Letter!**
TEC61032

**"Ssssend" Me a Letter!**
TEC61032

**"Ssssend" Me a Letter!**
TEC61032

**"Ssssend" Me a Letter!**
TEC61032

**"Ssssend" Me a Letter!**
TEC61032

**"Ssssend" Me a Letter!**
TEC61032

**"Ssssend" Me a Letter!**
TEC61032

# Sunny-Day Fun

### Pages 29–36

## Materials:

scissors
glue
paper clip
pencil
10" x 13" envelope
resealable plastic bag

## Preparing the center:

1. Tear out the student directions, center mat, and center cards on pages 31–36.
2. Glue the student directions (page 31) on the envelope. If desired, laminate the center mat and cards on pages 33–36.
3. Cut out the cards and place them in the bag.
4. Make copies of the recording sheet on page 30.
5. Store inside the envelope the center mat, bag, copies of the recording sheet, and a pencil and paper clip to make a spinner.

Subtracting two-digit numbers without regrouping

## Sunny-Day Fun

Remember to put the largest number on top.

# Sunny-Day Fun

## Here's what you do:

1. Put a card on the mat.

2. Use the pencil and paper clip to make a spinner.

3. Spin.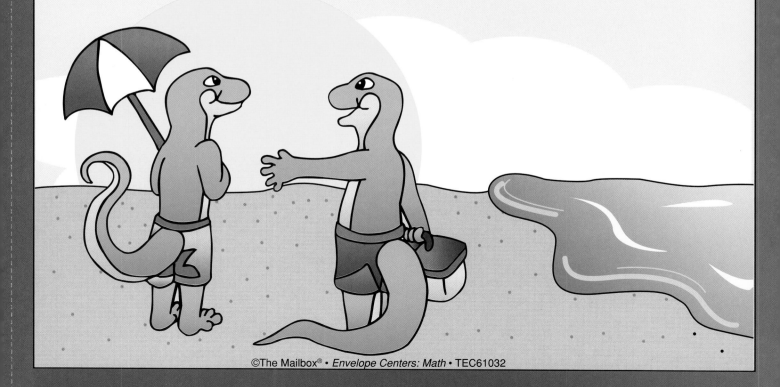

4. Use the number to write and solve the math problem on the recording sheet.

5. Replace the card and repeat.

Sunny-Day Fun

# Sunny-Day Fun

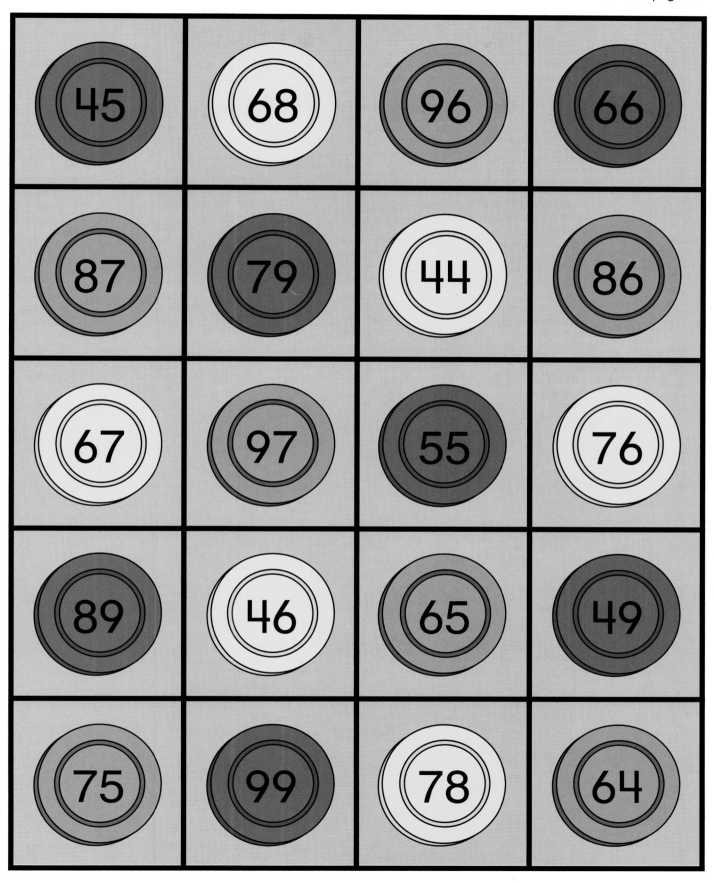

Sunny-Day Fun
TEC61032

Sunny-Day Fun
TEC61032

Sunny-Day Fun
TEC61032

Sunny-Day Fun
TEC61032

Sunny-Day Fun
TEC61032

Sunny-Day Fun
TEC61032

Sunny-Day Fun
TEC61032

Sunny-Day Fun
TEC61032

Sunny-Day Fun
TEC61032

Sunny-Day Fun
TEC61032

Sunny-Day Fun
TEC61032

Sunny-Day Fun
TEC61032

Sunny-Day Fun
TEC61032

Sunny-Day Fun
TEC61032

Sunny-Day Fun
TEC61032

Sunny-Day Fun
TEC61032

Sunny-Day Fun
TEC61032

Sunny-Day Fun
TEC61032

Sunny-Day Fun
TEC61032

Sunny-Day Fun
TEC61032

# Cleanup Crew

## Pages 37–44

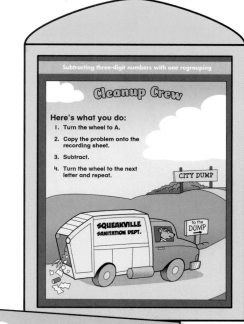

**Cleanup Crew**

**Here's what you do:**

1. Turn the wheel to A.
2. Copy the problem onto the recording sheet.
3. Subtract.
4. Turn the wheel to the next letter and repeat.

CITY DUMP

SQUEAKVILLE SANITATION DEPT.

to the DUMP

### Materials:

scissors
glue
brass fastener
10" x 13" envelope

### Preparing the center:

1. Tear out the student directions, center mat, and center wheel on pages 39–44. Laminate if desired.
2. Glue the student directions (page 39) on the envelope.
3. Cut out the wheel. Cut out the window on the center mat. Use the brass fastener to attach the wheel to the mat.
4. Make copies of the reproducible recording sheet on page 38.
5. Store the center mat and copies of the recording sheet inside the envelope. If desired, also include a copy of the answer key card on page 126 for self-checking.

**Cleanup Crew**

A. 763
  − 248

Name Max

Subtracting three-digit numbers with one regrouping

**Cleanup Crew**

| A. 763 −248 515 | B. | C. | D. | E. |
| F. | G. | H. | I. | J. |

# Cleanup Crew

| A. $-$ | B. $-$ | C. $-$ | D. $-$ | E. $-$ |
|---|---|---|---|---|
| F. $-$ | G. $-$ | H. $-$ | I. $-$ | J. $-$ |

**Note to the teacher:** Use with the directions on page 37.

# Cleanup Crew

## Here's what you do:

1. Turn the wheel to A.

2. Copy the problem onto the recording sheet.

3. Subtract.

4. Turn the wheel to the next letter and repeat.

CITY DUMP

SQUEAKVILLE SANITATION DEPT.

to the DUMP →

# Cleanup Crew

# Cleanup Crew

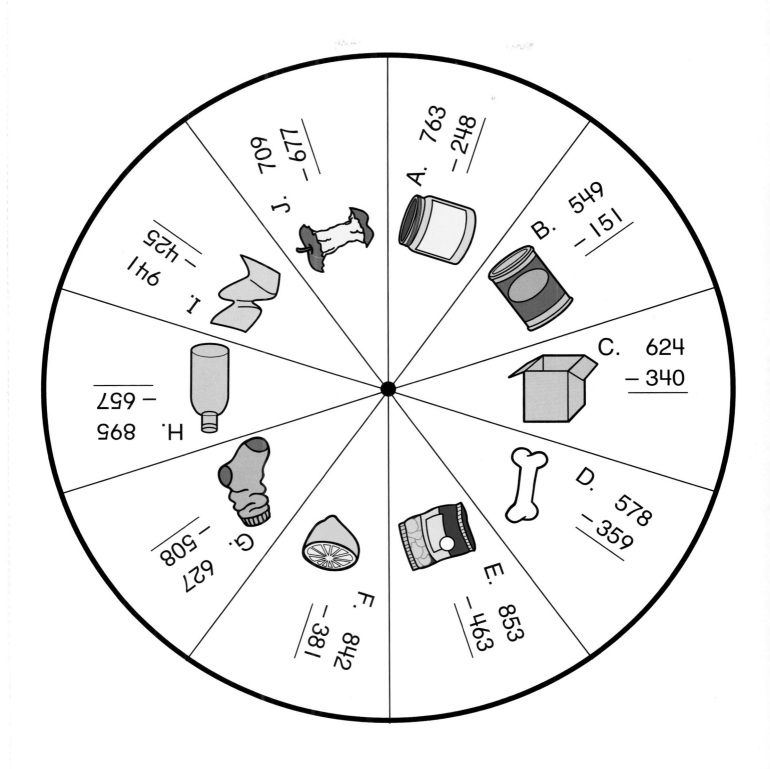

A. 763
 − 248

B. 549
 − 151

C. 624
 − 340

D. 578
 − 359

E. 853
 − 463

F. 842
 − 381

G. 627
 − 508

H. 895
 − 657

I. 941
 − 425

J. 709
 − 677

44

**Cleanup Crew**
TEC61032

# Cricket's Cupcakes

**Pages 45–52**

## Materials:

scissors
glue
10" x 13" envelope
resealable plastic bag

## Preparing the center:

1. Tear out the student directions, center mat, and center cards on pages 47–52.
2. Glue the student directions (page 47) on the envelope. If desired, laminate the center mat and cards on pages 49–52.
3. Cut out the cards and place them in the bag.
4. Make copies of the recording sheet on page 46.
5. Store the center mat, bag, and copies of the recording sheet inside the envelope. If desired, also include a copy of the answer key card on page 126 for self-checking.

Name _____

**46**

# Cricket's Cupcakes

Write each problem on the cupcake that matches its product.

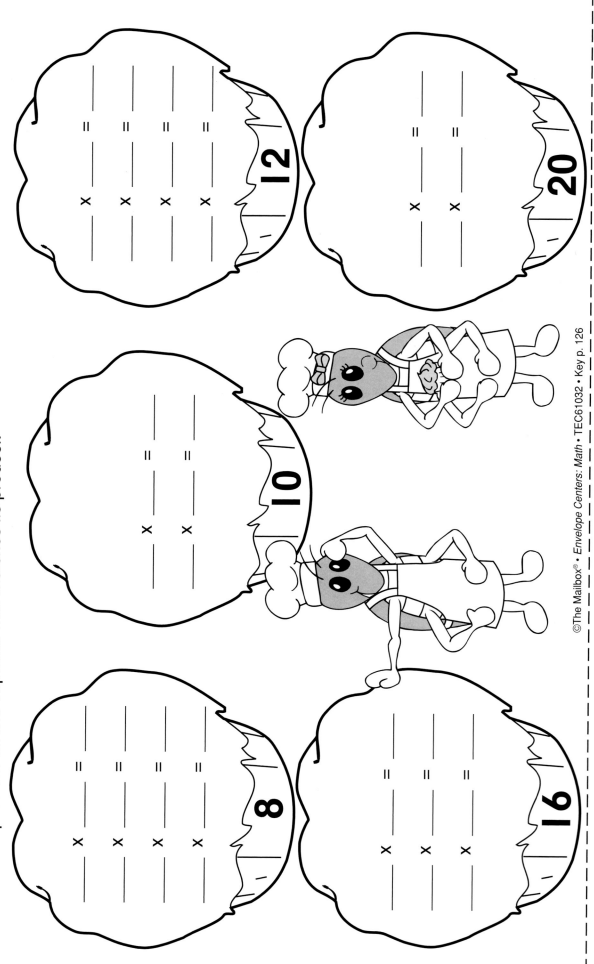

**Note to the teacher:** Use with the directions on page 45.

# Cricket's Cupcakes

## Here's what you do:

1. Multiply.

2. Put the card on the cupcake that matches its product.

3. Write the problem on the recording sheet.

4. Repeat.

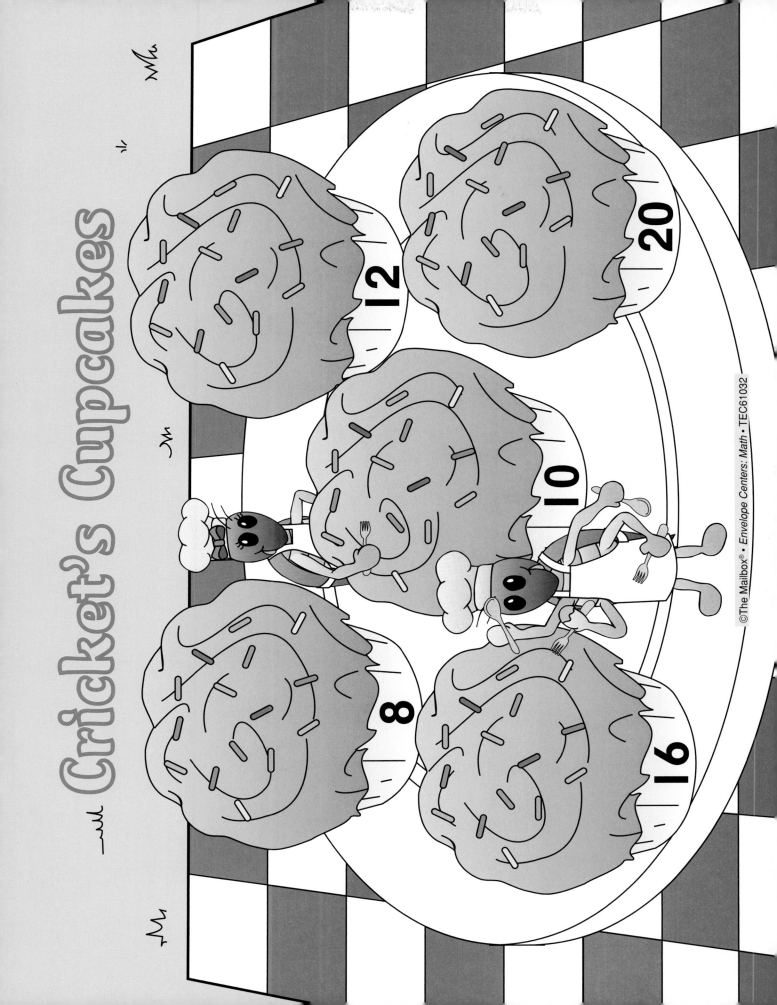

# Cricket's Cupcakes

| | | |
|---|---|---|
| 2 x 5 | 8 x 1 | 3 x 4 |
| 5 x 2 | 2 x 4 | 4 x 3 |
| 4 x 5 | 4 x 2 | 2 x 8 |
| 5 x 4 | 2 x 6 | 8 x 2 |
| 1 x 8 | 6 x 2 | 4 x 4 |

Cricket's Cupcakes
TEC61032

Cricket's Cupcakes
TEC61032

Cricket's Cupcakes
TEC61032

Cricket's Cupcakes
TEC61032

Cricket's Cupcakes
TEC61032

Cricket's Cupcakes
TEC61032

Cricket's Cupcakes
TEC61032

Cricket's Cupcakes
TEC61032

Cricket's Cupcakes
TEC61032

Cricket's Cupcakes
TEC61032

Cricket's Cupcakes
TEC61032

Cricket's Cupcakes
TEC61032

Cricket's Cupcakes
TEC61032

Cricket's Cupcakes
TEC61032

Cricket's Cupcakes
TEC61032

# Team Photo

**Pages 53–60**

## Materials:

scissors
glue
10" x 13" envelope
resealable plastic bag

## Preparing the center:

1. Tear out the student directions, center mat, and center cards on pages 55–60.
2. Glue the student directions (page 55) on the envelope. If desired, laminate the center mat and cards on pages 57–60.
3. Cut out the cards and place them in the bag.
4. Make copies of the recording sheet on page 54.
5. Store the center mat, bag, and copies of the recording sheet inside the envelope. If desired, also include a copy of the answer key card on page 126 for self-checking.

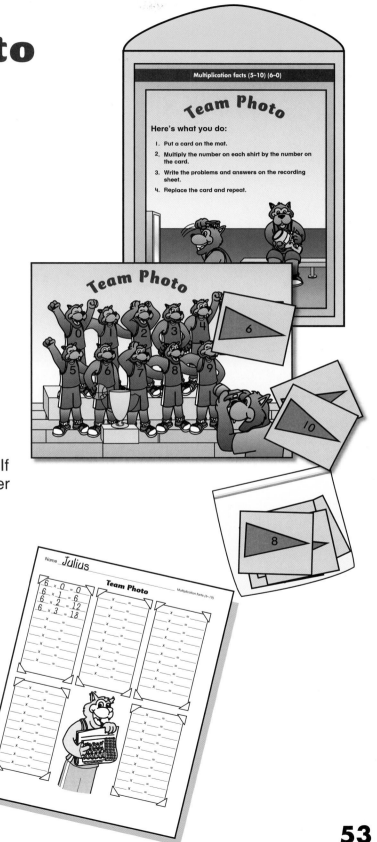

# Team Photo

| ___ X ___ = ___ | ___ X ___ = ___ | ___ X ___ = ___ |
| ___ X ___ = ___ | ___ X ___ = ___ | ___ X ___ = ___ |
| ___ X ___ = ___ | ___ X ___ = ___ | ___ X ___ = ___ |
| ___ X ___ = ___ | ___ X ___ = ___ | ___ X ___ = ___ |
| ___ X ___ = ___ | ___ X ___ = ___ | ___ X ___ = ___ |
| ___ X ___ = ___ | ___ X ___ = ___ | ___ X ___ = ___ |
| ___ X ___ = ___ | ___ X ___ = ___ | ___ X ___ = ___ |
| ___ X ___ = ___ | ___ X ___ = ___ | ___ X ___ = ___ |
| ___ X ___ = ___ | ___ X ___ = ___ | ___ X ___ = ___ |
| ___ X ___ = ___ | ___ X ___ = ___ | ___ X ___ = ___ |

| ___ X ___ = ___ | ___ X ___ = ___ |
| ___ X ___ = ___ | ___ X ___ = ___ |
| ___ X ___ = ___ | ___ X ___ = ___ |
| ___ X ___ = ___ | ___ X ___ = ___ |
| ___ X ___ = ___ | ___ X ___ = ___ |
| ___ X ___ = ___ | ___ X ___ = ___ |
| ___ X ___ = ___ | ___ X ___ = ___ |
| ___ X ___ = ___ | ___ X ___ = ___ |
| ___ X ___ = ___ | ___ X ___ = ___ |
| ___ X ___ = ___ | ___ X ___ = ___ |

**Note to the teacher:** Use with the directions on page 53.

# Team Photo

## Here's what you do:

1. Put a card on the mat.

2. Multiply the number on each shirt by the number on the card.

3. Write the problems and answers on the recording sheet.

4. Replace the card and repeat.

# Team Photo

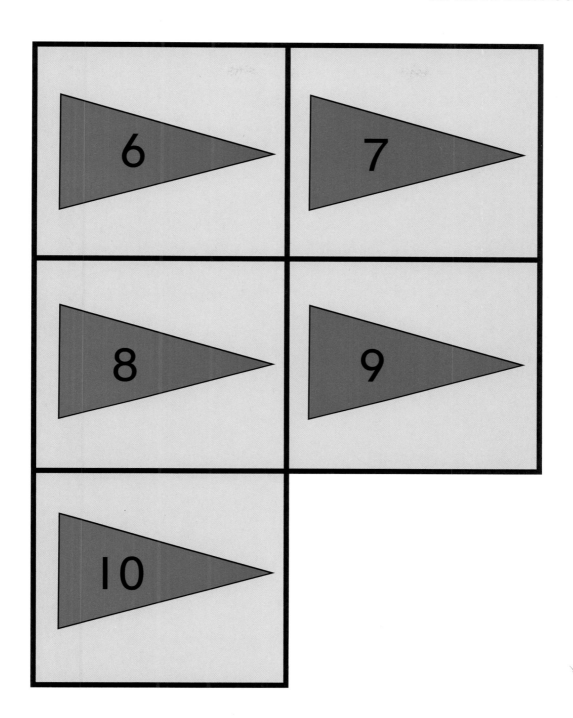

**Team Photo**
TEC61032

**Team Photo**
TEC61032

**Team Photo**
TEC61032

**Team Photo**
TEC61032

**Team Photo**
TEC61032

# Stocking Up

**Pages 61–68**

## Materials:

scissors
glue
10" x 13" envelope
2 resealable plastic bags

## Preparing the center:

1. Tear out the student directions, center mat, and center cards on pages 63–68.
2. Glue the student directions (page 63) on the envelope. If desired, laminate the center mat and cards on pages 65–68.
3. Cut out the cards and place each set in a separate bag.
4. Make copies of the recording sheet on page 62.
5. Store the center mat, bags, and copies of the recording sheet inside the envelope. If desired, also include a copy of the answer key card on page 126 for self-checking.

# Stocking Up

| | |
|---|---|
| A. <br><br> X _____ | B. <br><br> X _____ |
| C. <br><br> X _____ | D. <br><br> X _____ |

| | |
|---|---|
| E. <br><br> X _____ | F. <br><br> X _____ |
| G. <br><br> X _____ | H. <br><br> X _____ |

| | |
|---|---|
| I. <br><br> X _____ | J. <br><br> X _____ |
| K. <br><br> X _____ | L. <br><br> X _____ |

**Note to the teacher:** Use with the directions on page 61.

# Stocking Up

**Here's what you do:**

1. Copy problem A onto the recording sheet.

2. Multiply.

3. Put the card on the matching box.

4. Repeat with the remaining cards.

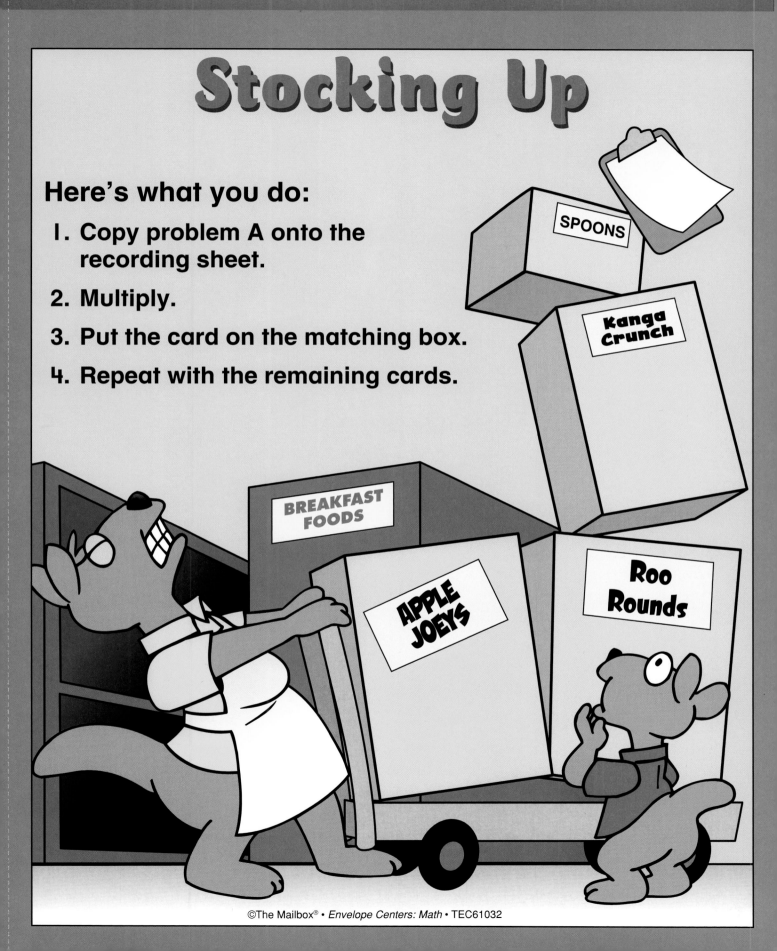

# Stocking Up

| Kanga Crunch | Kanga Crunch | Kanga Crunch | Kanga Crunch |
|---|---|---|---|
| 120 | 252 | 78 | 90 |

| Roo Rounds | Roo Rounds | Roo Rounds | Roo Rounds |
|---|---|---|---|
| 55 | 336 | 176 | 54 |

| APPLE JOEYS | APPLE JOEYS | APPLE JOEYS | APPLE JOEYS |
|---|---|---|---|
| 65 | 138 | 480 | 234 |

# Stocking Up

## Set 1

| | | | |
|---|---|---|---|
| A. 24 x 5 | B. 18 x 3 | C. 23 x 6 | D. 39 x 2 |
| E. 22 x 8 | F. 15 x 6 | G. 80 x 6 | H. 55 x 1 |
| I. 26 x 9 | J. 13 x 5 | K. 42 x 8 | L. 63 x 4 |

## Set 2

| | | | |
|---|---|---|---|
| A. 30 x 3 | B. 26 x 3 | C. 46 x 3 | D. 56 x 6 |
| E. 60 x 8 | F. 39 x 6 | G. 42 x 6 | H. 27 x 2 |
| I. 65 x 1 | J. 11 x 5 | K. 44 x 4 | L. 40 x 3 |

Stocking Up
TEC61032

Stocking Up
TEC61032

Stocking Up
TEC61032

Stocking Up
TEC61032

Stocking Up
TEC61032

Stocking Up
TEC61032

Stocking Up
TEC61032

Stocking Up
TEC61032

Stocking Up
TEC61032

Stocking Up
TEC61032

Stocking Up
TEC61032

Stocking Up
TEC61032

Stocking Up
TEC61032

Stocking Up
TEC61032

Stocking Up
TEC61032

Stocking Up
TEC61032

Stocking Up
TEC61032

Stocking Up
TEC61032

Stocking Up
TEC61032

Stocking Up
TEC61032

Stocking Up
TEC61032

Stocking Up
TEC61032

Stocking Up
TEC61032

Stocking Up
TEC61032

# What a Ride!

### Pages 69–76

## Materials:

scissors
glue
10" x 13" envelope
resealable plastic bag

## Preparing the center:

1. Tear out the student directions, center mat, and center cards on pages 71–76.
2. Glue the student directions (page 71) on the envelope. If desired, laminate the center mat and cards on pages 73–76.
3. Cut out the cards and place them in the bag.
4. Make copies of the recording sheet on page 70.
5. Store the center mat, bag, and copies of the recording sheet inside the envelope. If desired, also include a copy of the answer key card on page 127 for self-checking.

# What a Ride!

A.

_____ X _____ = _____

_____ ÷ _____ = _____

B.

_____ X _____ = _____

_____ ÷ _____ = _____

C.

_____ X _____ = _____

_____ ÷ _____ = _____

D.

_____ X _____ = _____

_____ ÷ _____ = _____

E.

_____ X _____ = _____

_____ ÷ _____ = _____

F.

_____ X _____ = _____

_____ ÷ _____ = _____

G.

_____ X _____ = _____

_____ ÷ _____ = _____

H.

_____ X _____ = _____

_____ ÷ _____ = _____

**Note to the teacher:** Use with the directions on page 69.

# What a Ride!

## Here's what you do:

1. Put a red fact card on the car.

2. Find the related blue fact card and place it on the car.

3. Write the facts on the recording sheet.

4. Repeat.

# What a Ride!

| | |
|---|---|
| $4 \times 8 = 32$ | $8 \times 3 = 24$ |
| $3 \times 7 = 21$ | $7 \times 4 = 28$ |
| $2 \times 6 = 12$ | $6 \times 5 = 30$ |
| $1 \times 9 = 9$ | $5 \times 2 = 10$ |

| | |
|---|---|
| $32 \div 4 = 8$ | $24 \div 8 = 3$ |
| $21 \div 3 = 7$ | $28 \div 7 = 4$ |
| $12 \div 2 = 6$ | $30 \div 6 = 5$ |
| $9 \div 9 = 1$ | $10 \div 5 = 2$ |

**What a Ride!**
TEC61032

**What a Ride!**
TEC61032

**What a Ride!**
TEC61032

**What a Ride!**
TEC61032

**What a Ride!**
TEC61032

**What a Ride!**
TEC61032

**What a Ride!**
TEC61032

**What a Ride!**
TEC61032

**What a Ride!**
TEC61032

**What a Ride!**
TEC61032

**What a Ride!**
TEC61032

**What a Ride!**
TEC61032

# What's for Lunch?

## Pages 77–84

### Materials:

scissors
glue
10" x 13" envelope
resealable plastic bag

### Preparing the center:

1. Tear out the student directions, center mat, and center cards on pages 79–84.
2. Glue the student directions (page 79) on the envelope. If desired, laminate the center mat and cards on pages 81–84.
3. Cut out the cards and place them in the bag.
4. Make copies of the recording sheet on page 78.
5. Store the center mat, bag, and copies of the recording sheet inside the envelope. If desired, also include a copy of the answer key card on page 127 for self-checking.

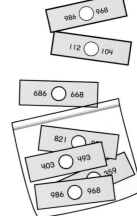

Name _____

# What's for Lunch?

A. ⬤

B. ⬤

C. ⬤

D. ⬤

E. ⬤

F. ⬤

G. ⬤

H. ⬤

I. ⬤

J. ⬤

K. ⬤

L. ⬤

**Note to the teacher:** Use with the directions on page 77.

# What's for Lunch?

## Here's what you do:

1. Put card A on the correct tray.

2. Write the number sentence on the recording sheet.

3. Repeat with the remaining cards.

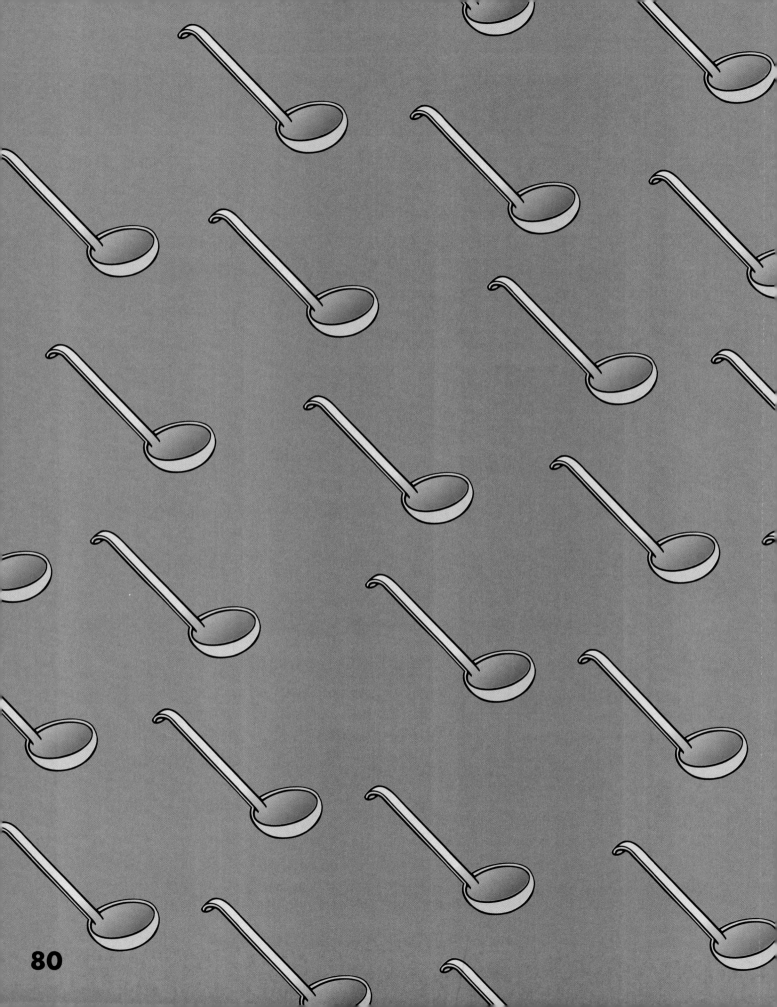

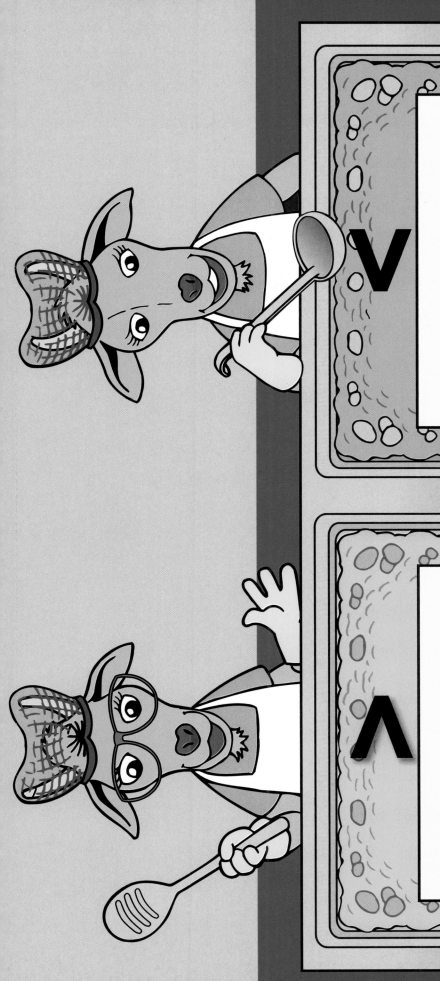

Less Than

Greater Than

What's for Lunch?

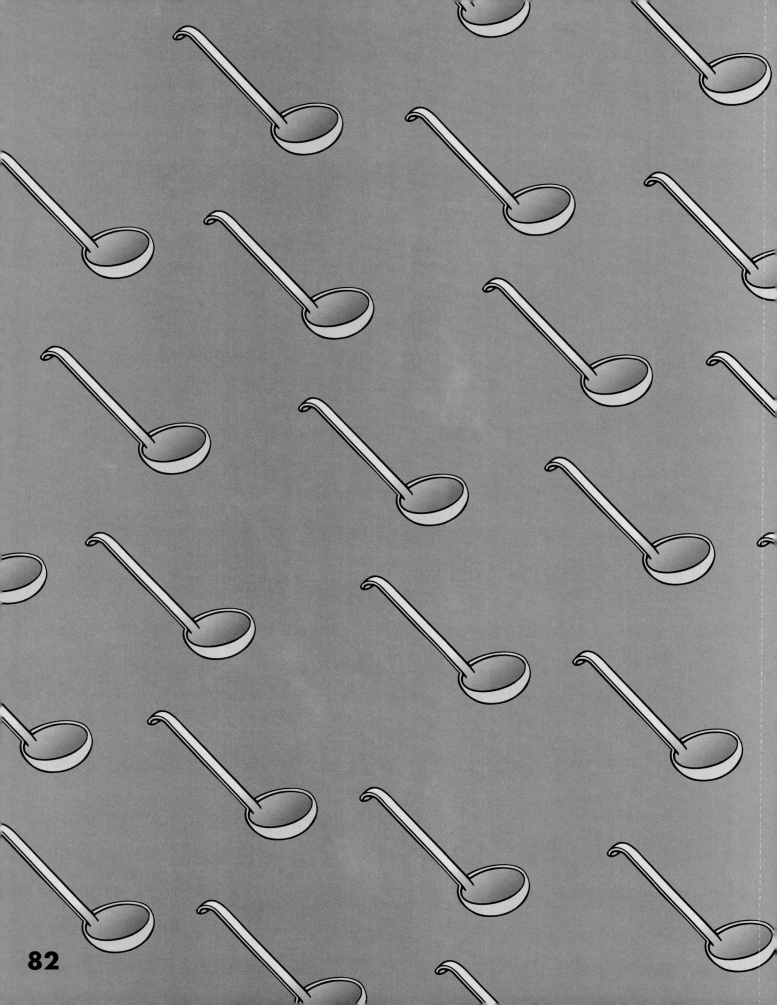

# What's for Lunch?

**Center Cards**
Use with the directions on page 77.

| | |
|---|---|
| A. 437 ◯ 743 | B. 686 ◯ 668 |
| C. 112 ◯ 104 | D. 359 ◯ 351 |
| E. 403 ◯ 493 | F. 724 ◯ 574 |
| G. 821 ◯ 831 | H. 527 ◯ 279 |
| I. 890 ◯ 908 | J. 536 ◯ 568 |
| K. 260 ◯ 265 | L. 986 ◯ 968 |

**What's for Lunch?**
TEC61032

**What's for Lunch?**
TEC61032

**What's for Lunch?**
TEC61032

**What's for Lunch?**
TEC61032

**What's for Lunch?**
TEC61032

**What's for Lunch?**
TEC61032

**What's for Lunch?**
TEC61032

**What's for Lunch?**
TEC61032

**What's for Lunch?**
TEC61032

**What's for Lunch?**
TEC61032

**What's for Lunch?**
TEC61032

**What's for Lunch?**
TEC61032

# Surf's Up!

### Pages 85–92

## Materials:

scissors
glue
10" x 13" envelope
2 resealable plastic bags

## Preparing the center:

1. Tear out the student directions, center mat, and center cards on pages 87–92.
2. Glue the student directions (page 87) on the envelope. If desired, laminate the center mat and cards on pages 89–92.
3. Cut out the cards and place each set in a separate bag.
4. Make copies of the recording sheet on page 86.
5. Store the center mat, bags, and copies of the recording sheet inside the envelope. If desired, also include a copy of the answer key card on page 127 to use for self-checking.

# Surf's Up!

**Hundreds**

**Tens**

**Ones**

**Note to the teacher:** Use with the directions on page 85.

## Here's what you do:

1. Choose one set of cards.

2. Sort the cards by the place value of the underlined digits.

3. Write the numbers on the recording sheet.

Surf's Up!

Ones

Tens

Hundreds

# Surf's Up!

| | |
|---|---|
| 19<u>6</u> | 45<u>2</u> |
| 3<u>9</u>5 | <u>1</u>43 |
| <u>8</u>21 | 18<u>0</u> |
| 37<u>5</u> | 6<u>4</u>5 |
| <u>7</u>96 | <u>5</u>07 |
| 2<u>0</u>0 | 9<u>3</u>0 |

| | |
|---|---|
| 8<u>1</u>2 | 96<u>1</u> |
| <u>2</u>35 | <u>6</u>90 |
| 72<u>3</u> | 4<u>5</u>8 |
| 3<u>6</u>9 | <u>9</u>07 |
| 80<u>4</u> | 58<u>8</u> |
| <u>4</u>44 | 1<u>7</u>6 |

Surf's Up!
TEC61032

Surf's Up!
TEC61032

Surf's Up!
TEC61032

Surf's Up!
TEC61032

Surf's Up!
TEC61032

Surf's Up!
TEC61032

Surf's Up!
TEC61032

Surf's Up!
TEC61032

Surf's Up!
TEC61032

Surf's Up!
TEC61032

Surf's Up!
TEC61032

Surf's Up!
TEC61032

Surf's Up!
TEC61032

Surf's Up!
TEC61032

Surf's Up!
TEC61032

Surf's Up!
TEC61032

Surf's Up!
TEC61032

Surf's Up!
TEC61032

Surf's Up!
TEC61032

Surf's Up!
TEC61032

Surf's Up!
TEC61032

Surf's Up!
TEC61032

Surf's Up!
TEC61032

Surf's Up!
TEC61032

# Dinner for Two

**Pages 93–100**

## Materials:

scissors
glue
10" x 13" envelope
resealable plastic bag

## Preparing the center:

1. Tear out the student directions, center mat, and center cards on pages 95–100.
2. Glue the student directions (page 95) on the envelope. If desired, laminate the center mat and cards on pages 97–100.
3. Cut out the cards and place them in the bag.
4. Make copies of the recording sheet on page 94.
5. Store the center mat, bag, and copies of the recording sheet inside the envelope. If desired, also include a copy of the answer key card on page 127 for self-checking.

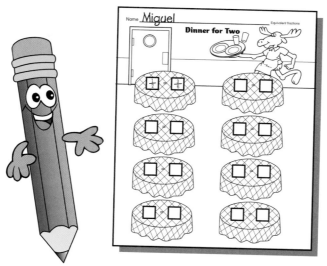

# Dinner for Two

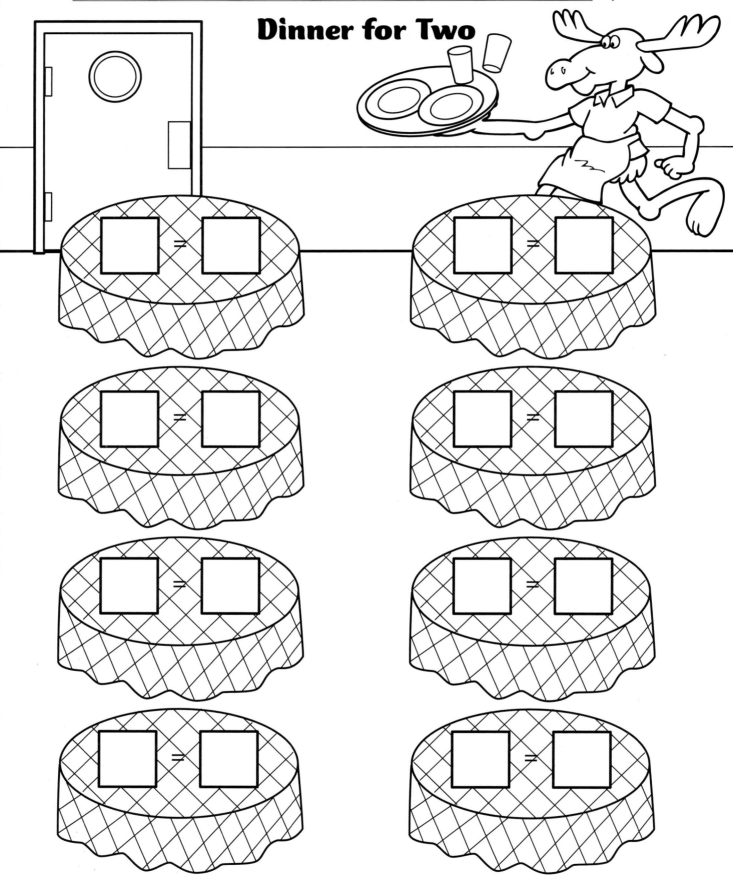

**Note to the teacher:** Use with the directions on page 93.

# Dinner for Two

## Here's what you do:

1. Put a fraction card on the table.

2. Find the equivalent fraction card and put it on the table.

3. Write the fraction pair on the recording sheet.

4. Repeat.

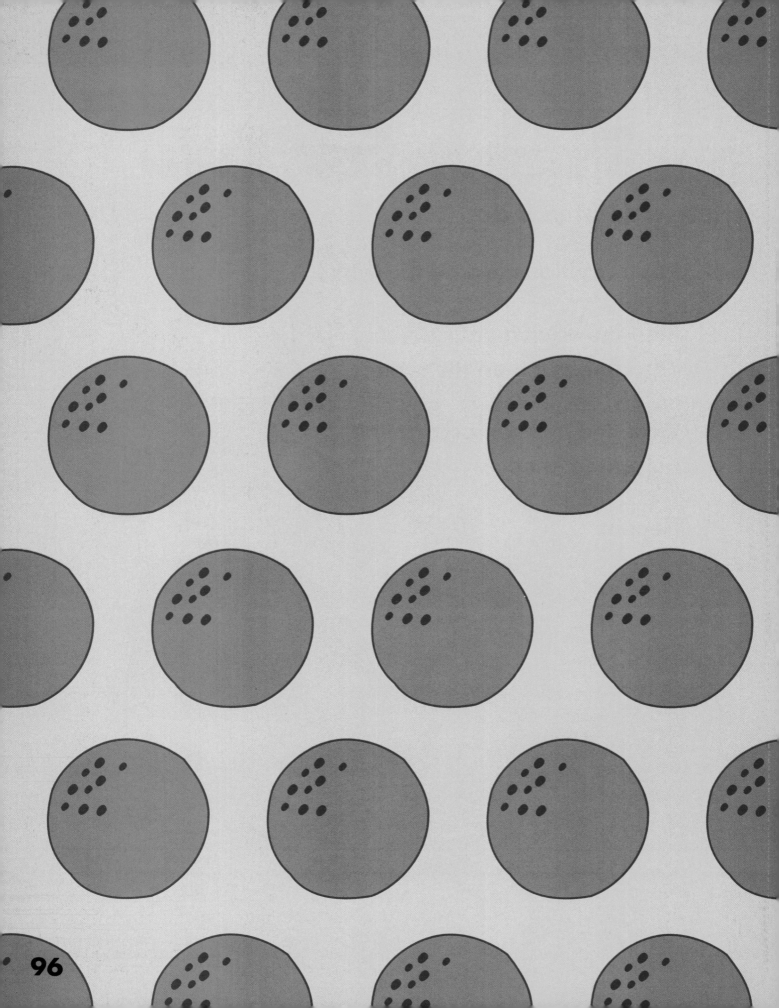

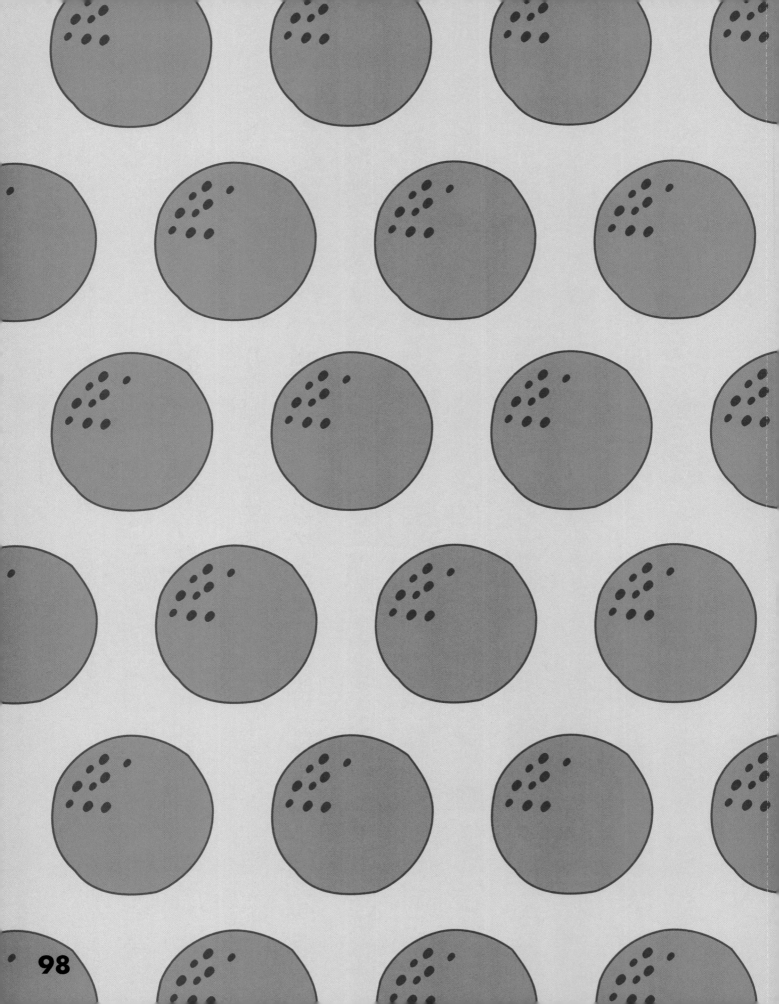

# Dinner for Two

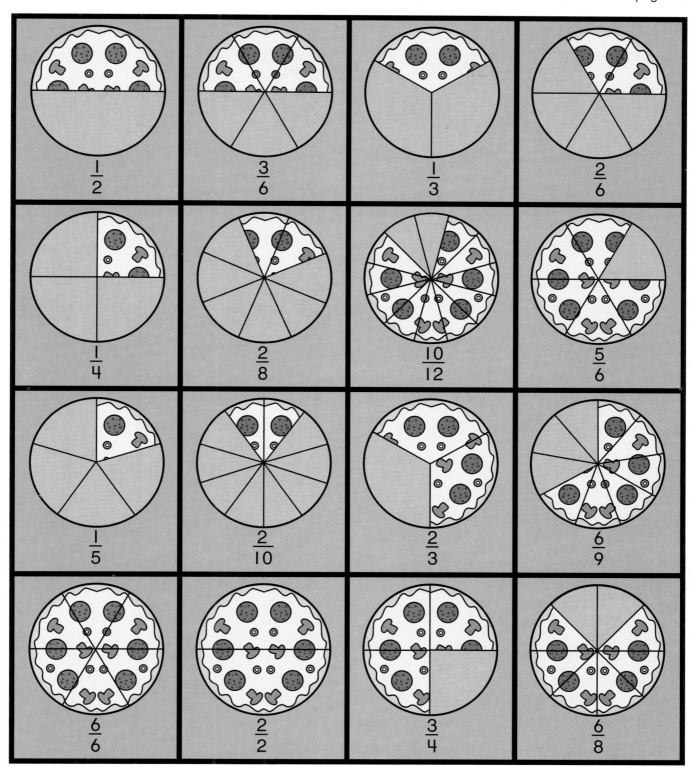

Dinner for Two
TEC61032

Dinner for Two
TEC61032

Dinner for Two
TEC61032

Dinner for Two
TEC61032

Dinner for Two
TEC61032

Dinner for Two
TEC61032

Dinner for Two
TEC61032

Dinner for Two
TEC61032

Dinner for Two
TEC61032

Dinner for Two
TEC61032

Dinner for Two
TEC61032

Dinner for Two
TEC61032

Dinner for Two
TEC61032

Dinner for Two
TEC61032

Dinner for Two
TEC61032

Dinner for Two
TEC61032

# Money Tree

### Pages 101–108

## Materials:

scissors
glue
10" x 13" envelope
resealable plastic bag
paper clip
pencil

## Preparing the center:

1. Tear out the student directions, center mat, and center cards on pages 103–108.
2. Glue the student directions (page 103) on the envelope. If desired, laminate the center mat and cards on pages 105–108.
3. Cut out the cards and place them in the bag.
4. Make copies of the recording sheet on page 102.
5. Store the center mat, bag, paper clip, pencil, and copies of the recording sheet inside the envelope.

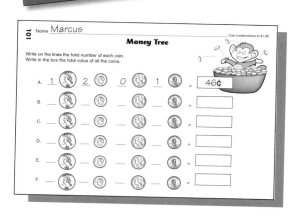

# Money Tree

Coin combinations to $1.00

Write on the lines the total number of each coin.
Write in the box the total value of all the coins.

| | | | | |
|---|---|---|---|---|
| A. |  ____ |  ____ |  ____ |  ____ = ☐ |
| B. | ____ | ____ | ____ | ____ = ☐ |
| C. | ____ | ____ | ____ | ____ = ☐ |
| D. | ____ | ____ | ____ | ____ = ☐ |
| E. | ____ | ____ | ____ | ____ = ☐ |
| F. | ____ | ____ | ____ | ____ = ☐ |

Note to the teacher: Use with the directions on page 101.

# Money Tree

## Here's what you do:

1. Spin the paper clip and place the matching coin on the basket.

2. Repeat three more times.

3. Record the four coins and their total value on the recording sheet.

4. Remove the coins from the basket.

5. Repeat.

# Money Tree

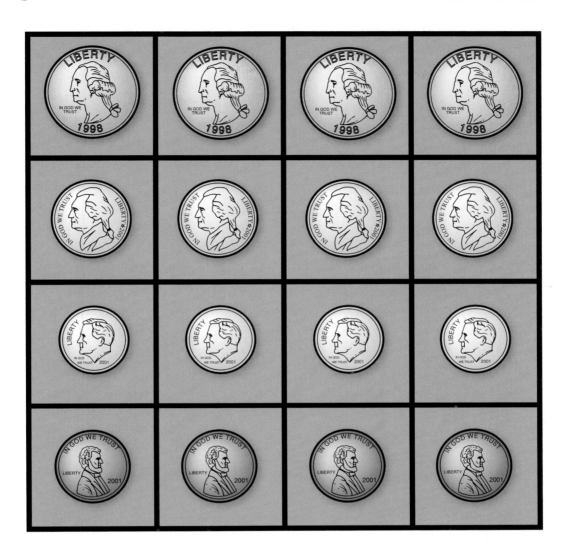

Money Tree
**TEC61032**

Money Tree
TEC61032

Money Tree
TEC61032

Money Tree
TEC61032

Money Tree
TEC61032

Money Tree
TEC61032

Money Tree
TEC61032

Money Tree
TEC61032

Money Tree
TEC61032

Money Tree
TEC61032

Money Tree
TEC61032

Money Tree
TEC61032

Money Tree
TEC61032

Money Tree
TEC61032

Money Tree
TEC61032

Money Tree
TEC61032

# Tee Time

## Pages 109–116

### Materials:

scissors
glue
10" x 13" envelope
2 resealable plastic bags
brad

### Preparing the center:

1. Tear out the student directions, center mat, center cards, and clock hands on pages 111–116.
2. Glue the student directions (page 111) on the envelope. If desired, laminate the center mat, cards, and clock hands on pages 113–116.
3. Cut out the cards and the clock hands. Place each set of cards in a separate bag. Attach the clock hands to the center mat with a brad.
4. Make copies of the recording sheet on page 110.
5. Store the center mat, bags, and copies of the recording sheet inside the envelope. If desired, also include a copy of the answer key card on page 128 for self-checking.

# Tee Time

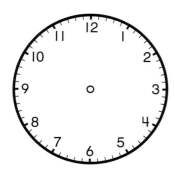

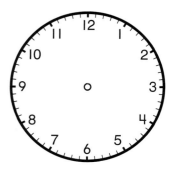

A. ____ : ____     B. ____ : ____     C. ____ : ____     D. ____ : ____

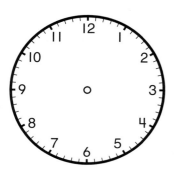
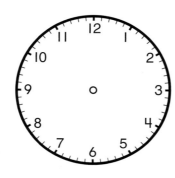
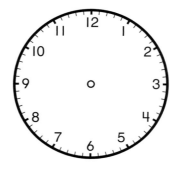
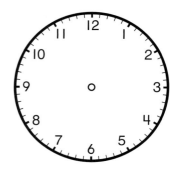

E. ____ : ____     F. ____ : ____     G. ____ : ____     H. ____ : ____

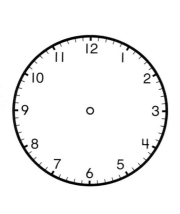
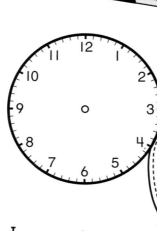

I. ____ : ____     J. ____ : ____

©The Mailbox® • *Envelope Centers: Math* • TEC61032 • Key p. 128

**110**   **Note to the teacher:** Use with the directions on page 109.

# Tee Time

## Here's what you do:

1. Put card A on the mat.

2. Show the time on the clock.

3. Draw the hands on the recording sheet and write the time.

4. Repeat with the remaining cards.

# Tee Time

## Time to the quarter hour

| F. 5:45 | G. 6:45 | H. 8:45 | I. 1:45 | J. 4:45 |
| --- | --- | --- | --- | --- |
| A. 3:15 | B. 7:15 | C. 9:15 | D. 11:15 | E. 12:15 |

## Time to the half hour

| F. 9:30 | G. 10:30 | H. 3:30 | I. 12:30 | J. 5:30 |
| --- | --- | --- | --- | --- |
| A. 1:00 | B. 2:00 | C. 4:00 | D. 6:00 | E. 7:00 |

minute hand

hour hand

Tee Time
TEC61032

Tee Time
TEC61032

Tee Time
TEC61032

Tee Time
TEC61032

Tee Time
TEC61032

Tee Time
TEC61032

Tee Time
TEC61032

Tee Time
TEC61032

Tee Time
TEC61032

Tee Time
TEC61032

Tee Time
TEC61032

Tee Time
TEC61032

Tee Time
TEC61032

Tee Time
TEC61032

Tee Time
TEC61032

Tee Time
TEC61032

Tee Time
TEC61032

Tee Time
TEC61032

Tee Time
TEC61032

Tee Time
TEC61032

# Camp Big Bear

## Pages 117–124

### Materials:

scissors
glue
10" x 13" envelope

### Preparing the center:

1. Tear out the student directions, center mat, center card, and ruler on pages 119–124.
2. Glue the student directions (page 119) on the envelope. If desired, laminate the center mat, card, and ruler on pages 121–124.
3. Cut out the center card and ruler.
4. Make copies of the recording sheet on page 118.
5. Store the center mat, card, ruler, and copies of the recording sheet inside the envelope. If desired, also include a copy of the answer key card on page 128 for self-checking.

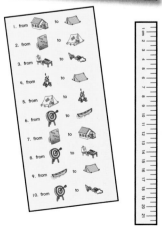

Measuring to the nearest centimeter _____

# Camp Big Bear

ruler: cm 1 2 3 4 5 6 7 8 9 10 11 12 13 14 15

1. _____ cm

2. _____ cm

3. _____ cm

4. _____ cm

5. _____ cm

6. _____ cm

7. _____ cm

8. _____ cm

9. _____ cm

10. _____ cm

©The Mailbox® • *Envelope Centers: Math* • TEC61032 • Key p. 128

**Note to the teacher:** Use with the directions on page 117.

# Camp Big Bear

## Here's what you do:

1. Read the first clue on the card.

2. Use your ruler to measure from dot to dot to the nearest centimeter.

3. Write the distance on the recording sheet.

4. Repeat.

# Camp Big Bear

• rock climbing wall

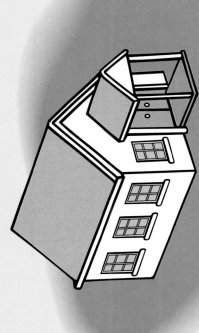

• dining hall

• campfire

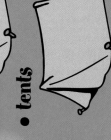

• tents

• arts and crafts

• bird study

• first aid

• archery

• water sports

# Camp Big Bear

1. from ⌂ to ⛺
2. from ⬜ to ⛺
3. from 🖼 to 🐦
4. from 🔥 to ⛺
5. from ⛺ to 🔥
6. from 🎯 to 🛶
7. from ⬜ to ⌂
8. from 🎯 to 🖼
9. from 🛶 to ⛺
10. from 🎯 to 🐦

# Answer Keys

## Page 6: "Pajama Party"

**Strip 1**
A. 9 + 8 = 17
B. 12 − 8 = 4
C. 7 + 7 = 14
D. 11 − 6 = 5
E. 17 − 9 = 8
F. 9 + 7 = 16
G. 15 − 8 = 7
H. 10 − 7 = 3
I. 6 + 9 = 15
J. 9 + 9 = 18
K. 14 − 8 = 6
L. 7 + 5 = 12

**Strip 2**
A. 7 + 9 = 16
B. 14 − 7 = 7
C. 11 − 7 = 4
D. 8 + 7 = 15
E. 18 − 9 = 9
F. 5 + 6 = 11
G. 16 − 8 = 8
H. 9 + 5 = 14
I. 13 − 7 = 6
J. 6 + 6 = 12
K. 8 + 9 = 17
L. 15 − 6 = 9

## Page 22: "'Ssssend' Me a Letter!"

A. 601   B. 795   C. 819   D. 928

E. 963   F. 783   G. 647   H. 994

I. 869   J. 640   K. 947   L. 515

M. 808   N. 716   O. 872   P. 309

Q. 483   R. 519

S. 976   T. 916

## Page 14: "Pampered Pups"

A.   25
   + 43
     68

B.   37
   + 61
     98

C.   30
   + 40
     70

D.   84
   + 14
     98

E.   31
   + 56
     87

F.   25
   + 20
     45

G.   23
   + 71
     94

H.   41
   + 52
     93

I.   60
   + 15
     75

J.   21
   + 31
     52

K.   34
   + 20
     54

L.   54
   + 11
     65

M.   63
   + 33
     96

N.   21
   + 58
     79

O.   10
   + 40
     50

P.   46
   + 22
     68

Q.   12
   + 36
     48

R.   21
   + 15
     36

S.   50
   + 43
     93

T.   75
   + 23
     98

**Page 38: "Cleanup Crew:"**

A. 515     B. 398     C. 284     D. 219     E. 390

F. 461     G. 119     H. 238     I. 516     J. 32

**Page 46: "Cricket's Cupcakes"**
Order may vary.

| 8 | 10 | 12 |
|---|---|---|
| 1 x 8 = 8 | 2 x 5 = 10 | 2 x 6 = 12 |
| 8 x 1 = 8 | 5 x 2 = 10 | 6 x 2 = 12 |
| 2 x 4 = 8 | | 3 x 4 = 12 |
| 4 x 2 = 8 | | 4 x 3 = 12 |

| 16 | 20 |
|---|---|
| 2 x 8 = 16 | 4 x 5 = 20 |
| 8 x 2 = 16 | 5 x 4 = 20 |
| 4 x 4 = 16 | |

**Page 62: "Stocking Up"**
**Set 1**

A. 120     B. 54
C. 138     D. 78

E. 176     F. 90          I. 234     J. 65
G. 480     H. 55          K. 336     L. 252

**Set 2**

A. 90     B. 78
C. 138     D. 336

E. 480     F. 234          I. 65     J. 55
G. 252     H. 54          K. 176     L. 120

**Page 54: "Team Photo"**
Order may vary.

| | | |
|---|---|---|
| 6 x 0 = 0 | 7 x 0 = 0 | 8 x 0 = 0 |
| 6 x 1 = 6 | 7 x 1 = 7 | 8 x 1 = 8 |
| 6 x 2 = 12 | 7 x 2 = 14 | 8 x 2 = 16 |
| 6 x 3 = 18 | 7 x 3 = 21 | 8 x 3 = 24 |
| 6 x 4 = 24 | 7 x 4 = 28 | 8 x 4 = 32 |
| 6 x 5 = 30 | 7 x 5 = 35 | 8 x 5 = 40 |
| 6 x 6 = 36 | 7 x 6 = 42 | 8 x 6 = 48 |
| 6 x 7 = 42 | 7 x 7 = 49 | 8 x 7 = 56 |
| 6 x 8 = 48 | 7 x 8 = 56 | 8 x 8 = 64 |
| 6 x 9 = 54 | 7 x 9 = 63 | 8 x 9 = 72 |

| | |
|---|---|
| 9 x 0 = 0 | 10 x 0 = 0 |
| 9 x 1 = 9 | 10 x 1 = 10 |
| 9 x 2 = 18 | 10 x 2 = 20 |
| 9 x 3 = 27 | 10 x 3 = 30 |
| 9 x 4 = 36 | 10 x 4 = 40 |
| 9 x 5 = 45 | 10 x 5 = 50 |
| 9 x 6 = 54 | 10 x 6 = 60 |
| 9 x 7 = 63 | 10 x 7 = 70 |
| 9 x 8 = 72 | 10 x 8 = 80 |
| 9 x 9 = 81 | 10 x 9 = 90 |

**Page 70: "What a Ride!"**
Order may vary.

A. $1 \times 9 = 9$
   $9 \div 9 = 1$

B. $2 \times 6 = 12$
   $12 \div 2 = 6$

C. $3 \times 7 = 21$
   $21 \div 3 = 7$

D. $4 \times 8 = 32$
   $32 \div 4 = 8$

E. $5 \times 2 = 10$
   $10 \div 5 = 2$

F. $6 \times 5 = 30$
   $30 \div 6 = 5$

G. $7 \times 4 = 28$
   $28 \div 7 = 4$

H. $8 \times 3 = 24$
   $24 \div 8 = 3$

**Page 86: "Surf's Up!"**
**Pink**
Order of answers in each grouping may vary.

| Hundreds | Tens | Ones |
|---|---|---|
| 8<u>2</u>1 | 3<u>9</u>5 | 19<u>6</u> |
| <u>7</u>96 | <u>2</u>00 | 37<u>5</u> |
| <u>1</u>43 | 6<u>4</u>5 | 45<u>2</u> |
| <u>5</u>07 | 9<u>3</u>0 | 18<u>0</u> |

**Yellow**
Order of answers in each grouping may vary.

| Hundreds | Tens | Ones |
|---|---|---|
| <u>2</u>35 | 1<u>7</u>6 | 58<u>8</u> |
| <u>4</u>44 | 3<u>6</u>9 | 72<u>3</u> |
| <u>6</u>90 | 4<u>5</u>8 | 80<u>4</u> |
| <u>9</u>07 | 8<u>1</u>2 | 96<u>1</u> |

**Page 78: "What's for Lunch?"**

A. $437 < 743$

B. $686 > 668$

C. $112 > 104$

D. $359 > 351$

E. $403 < 493$

F. $724 > 574$

G. $821 < 831$

H. $527 > 279$

I. $890 < 908$

J. $536 < 568$

K. $260 < 265$

L. $986 > 968$

**Page 94: "Dinner for Two"**
Order may vary.

$\frac{1}{2} = \frac{3}{6}$    $\frac{1}{3} = \frac{2}{6}$

$\frac{1}{4} = \frac{2}{8}$    $\frac{10}{12} = \frac{5}{6}$

$\frac{1}{5} = \frac{2}{10}$    $\frac{2}{3} = \frac{6}{9}$

$\frac{6}{6} = \frac{2}{2}$    $\frac{3}{4} = \frac{6}{8}$

## Page 110: "Tee Time"
### Time to the Half Hour

A. 1:00

B. 2:00

C. 4:00

D. 6:00

E. 7:00

F. 9:30

G. 10:30

H. 3:30

I. 12:30

J. 5:30

### Time to the Quarter Hour

A. 3:15

B. 7:15

C. 9:15

D. 11:15

E. 12:15

F. 5:45

G. 6:45

H. 8:45

I. 1:45

J. 4:45

## Page 118: "Camp Big Bear"
### Finals

1. 10
2. 7
3. 11
4. 3
5. 13

6. 10
7. 11
8. 9
9. 19
10. 12